# Seasons of the
# FRESHWATER POND BiOME

Written by
Shirley Duke

Rourke
Educational Media
rourkeeducationalmedia.com

Scan for Related Titles
and Teacher Resources

www.rourkeeducationalmedia.com

PHOTO CREDITS: Cover: © Pavel Klimenko; page 4: © Antagain (frog), © kaniwi (beaver); page 5: © igor terekhov; page 6: © Mia Blake; page 7: © Bruce Smith; page 8: © scrabble2; page 9: © Michael G. Mill; page 10: © Stephen Strathdee; page 11: © John Anderson; page 12: © Ryan M. Bolton; page 13: © Andrew Roland; page 14: © Jitalia17; page 15: © Trevor Reeves, © bbtomas; page 16: © Julie Lubick; page 17: © Patrick Le; page 18: © Ken Rygh Creative Art & Design; page 19: © Phoric; page 20: © Stratum; page 21: © Steve Debenport

Edited by Precious McKenzie

Cover design by Renee Brady
Interior design by Tara Raymo

**Library of Congress PCN Data**

Seasons of the Freshwater Pond Biome / Shirley Duke
(Biomes)
ISBN 978-1-62169-899-9 (hard cover)
ISBN 978-1-62169-794-7 (soft cover)
ISBN 978-1-62717-006-2 (e-Book)
Library of Congress Control Number: 2013936815

Also Available as:

ROURKE'S
e-Books

Rourke Educational Media
Printed in the United States of America,
North Mankato, Minnesota

Rourke
Educational Media

rourkeeducationalmedia.com

customerservice@rourkeeducationalmedia.com  •  PO Box 643328 Vero Beach, Florida 32964

# Table of Contents

# Still and Small

What makes a **freshwater pond**? A pond forms when a **shallow** hole fills with rain or running water.

Freshwater Ponds have:

✓ Small freshwater source

✓ Birds, insects, and fish

✓ Algae

✓ Season like the area where they are found

Beavers are one of a few animals that can change the land where they live. They dam creeks to make ponds.

Ponds are not as deep or large as lakes. The small size of ponds **limits** the life found there.

# Seasons of Change

In spring, flowers pop open. Eggs hatch.
It's a time of life in the pond.

Tiny bugs move about. Birds return to nest. Frogs call at night.

In summer, bugs fly around the pond.

Fish grow and swim. Turtles sun on rocks.

Plants grow fast in the bright Sun. **Algae** often covers the pond.

In the fall, cool air comes. Berries ripen.
Birds fly south.

Turtles and frogs bury themselves in pond mud and sleep through the cold winter.

Winter brings more changes. The water is cold or even frozen. Animals hide in **dens** to stay warm.

# Water Plants and More

Tall, thin **cattails** and reeds rise above the shallow water. Bugs climb them and ducks and snails eat them.

Around ponds, grasses and flowers grow in the damp soil.

Some plants grow under water. Some plants float on top of the water. Plants also grow up from the water.

Algae and other plants too small to see
grow in ponds, too.

Crayfish move in the mud at the bottom of the pond.

Dead plant matter sinks in the pond. It **decays**, adding to the muddy bottom.

# Life at the Pond

Fish and snails eat the tiny plants and insects.
Frogs, turtles, and snakes call ponds home.

Raccoons catch and eat the small animals living at the pond. They mostly hunt at night.

Birds drop by for a snack. Ducks swim and dive. Animals stop to drink.

# The Future of Freshwater Ponds

People litter and harm ponds.

People can hurt ponds with their actions.

You can take care of the plants and animals that live in freshwater ponds near you.

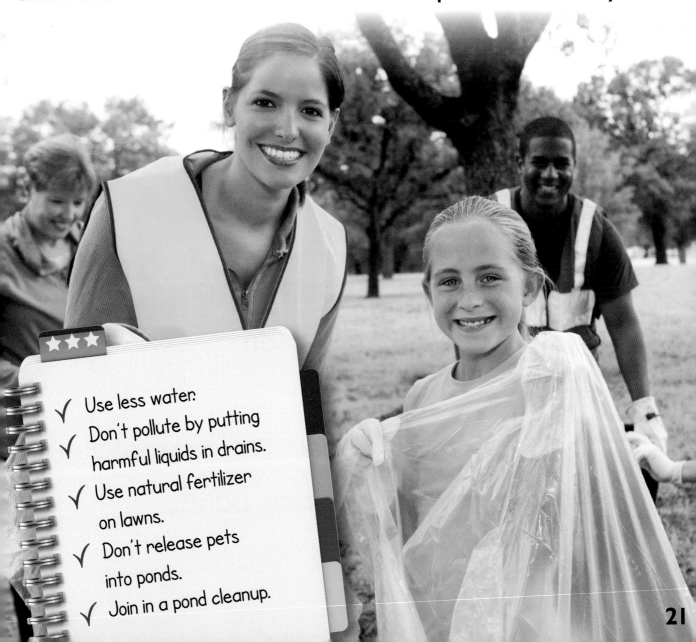

✓ Use less water.
✓ Don't pollute by putting harmful liquids in drains.
✓ Use natural fertilizer on lawns.
✓ Don't release pets into ponds.
✓ Join in a pond cleanup.

21

# Try This!
# Life Changes at the Pond

1. Go to a pond with an adult.

2. Look around.

3. List all the life you see.

4. Describe the plants and animals.

5. Visit the pond each season.


Did you see any changes? Writing what you see is one way people study ponds.

# Glossary

**algae** (AL-gee): a life form that can make food like a plant but has no roots or stem

**cattails** (KAT-tayls): tall, thin water plants with a furry, brown top

**decays** (di-KAYS): to rot or break down into smaller parts

**dens** (denz): the homes or burrows of wild animals

**freshwater pond** (FRESH-waw-tur PAHND): a small body of water that is not salt water

**limits** (LIM-its): the point that prevents anything more from being in a place

**shallow** (SHAL-oh): water that is not very deep

# Index

# Websites

www.fcps.edu/islandcreekes/ecology/pond.htm

www.msnucleus.org/membership/activities/pond2.html

kids.nceas.ucsb.edu/biomes/freshwater.html

# About the Author

Shirley Duke has written many books about science. She lives in Texas and New Mexico and loves the different seasons in each place. She has explored many different ponds and studied the fish and other life in them. She had great fun as a child using string and bacon to catch pond crayfish, known as crawdads in Texas.

Meet The Author!
www.meetREMauthors.com